HOLL NDMILLS

For centuries, which ever way you looked, there was always a windmill on the Dutch horizon. They were present on very old paintings and pictures. Jacob van Ruisdael, for instance, painted the picture, shown beside, between 1668 and 1682.

Wijk bij Duurstede, 17th century, painted by Jacob van Ruisdael

The mill stood on a defence tower in the city wall of Wijk bij Duurstede. This windmill was demolished in about the year 1810. Then for a long time, the Rijn and Lek windmill (1659) was thought to be the windmill which Jacob van Ruisdael had painted. The foot of this demolished windmill can still be seen. At the time windmills were built to supply power for the work to be done at the mill. As long as people have been growing corn for food, there has been a need to grind corn into flour.

This was done by primitive methods for centuries. First manually, then later the treadmill (horsepower) and watermill took over.
At a later stage the windmill was developed, which was very successful in our flat and windy country. This caused a greater demand for these mills which resulted in a favourable effect in relation to the technical development of the windmill. It is because of this that the windmill was used for many more purposes than just milling grain. They were used for hulling barley into pearl barley and groats, at that time almost a daily staple diet.
The windmills sawed logs into beams, boards and laths and produced paper. They crushed oil from oilseeds like linseed and rape. Spices were ground and mustard was made. The fulling mills converted fabrics into our famous cloths.

Hemp-pounders processed the stems of hemp in such a way that they could be used to make ropes and canvas. It is therefore understandable that

The Windmill, an etching by Rembrandt dating from 1641

many present day industries found their origin in the milling world. An example of this is the Zaan area where many of the mills formed the basis of the present industries in the area. Above all we should remember the fact that it was the mill that drained the large lakes called Beemster, Purmer and Schermer, and that until recently they regulated the water level of The Netherlands.

One can hardly imagine there was a time when the number of mills totalled 9,000. Now there are only just under a thousand windmills left. The reasons for this declining number are many, but the main reason is the coming of other new sources of motive power, the steam engine, the combustion engine and electric motors.

The small capacity of the mill as an industrial enterprise became uninteresting for many entrepreneurs, resulting in neglect.

'De Saen' in the year 1850, painted by Peter Sterkenburg

The Westbroek polder mills

Lightning followed by fire, strong gales and acts of war also played havoc with the windmills and the money and enthusiasm needed to rebuild them was then out of the question! Without a doubt, mills are the most vulnerable category of Dutch monuments.

Therefore it should be an important task for the authorities and the Dutch nation to ensure this minimum of roughly 1,000 remaining mills stays an absolute minimum. Many people have realised this and formed mill societies.

The most prominent of these is the Vereniging ***"De Hollandsche Molen"*** (Association *"The Dutch Windmill"*) which has been active since 1923 and the ***"Guild of Voluntary Millers"***.

The members of this guild keep the mills going, which otherwise would be condemned to a standstill, idleness and deterioration. The volunteers added the notion of *"Working"* to the sequence of *"Mills, Idle, Decay, Restore"*, because mills have to work, they were built for that purpose.

The Keukenhof mill

It is owing to them that Holland remains *"the Land of Windmills"*. It is also owing to them that we can remain witness to the essential role the mill plays in the Dutch scenery with its wide horizons and fascinating cloudy skies.

For you, reader, may this book be an educative introduction to our *"national trade mark"* and we hope that you will *"see"* and admire the mill as a monument of ingenuity and craftsmanship.

"Putmolen" in Aarlanderveen in the year 1801

Mills in Kinderdijk

Types of mills

One can distinguish between two types of mills: the watermills that are driven by the force of water and the windmills which, as the name suggests, are driven by the wind.

Watermill in Baarlo (Limburg)

The mill "De Huisman", Zaanse Schans

Bosmolen & Doeshofmolen, Leiderdorp

WATERMILLS

Watermill in Wijlre (Limburg)

Watermills are only to be found in the eastern and southern provinces, so in Twente, Oost-Veluwe, the Achterhoek, Oost-Brabant and Limburg. Thus in those places where there is a sufficient flow of water to drive the wheel of a mill.

There are three different types:

A. **Overshot mills,** where the water is guided along the top of the wheel.

B. **Breastshot mills,** where the water is guided near the middle of the wheel thus making it turn.

C. **Undershot mills,** where the running water hits the wheel underneath.

Usually these are corn mills, but in principle they could be used for other industrial purposes as in former times. (Producing paper, milling oilseeds, sawing timber, etc.).

There are about eighty of these watermills left in The Netherlands, the majority in Limburg.

Interior of a watermill in Oploo (Limburg)

Watermill, Grathem

Watermill, Arcen

Mallumsche watermill

Opwettense watermill near Nuenen (1743)

WINDMILLS

There is still a great variety of windmills. The names are rather complicated and stem from the construction, the appearance or function of the mill, or a combination of these factors. We will introduce you to the most prominent types:

Post-mill "De Vlijt", Gelfen

Post-mill, Uden (1811)

POST-MILL

Undoubtedly this is the oldest type of mill in our country and they were already used in or around the year 1200 as corn mills and they remained as such. The square mill house rests upon a strong vertical wooden spindle, the *"standard"* or post, on which post it has to be turned to face the wind. Strong quarter-bars keep the standard in its vertical position as well. The foundations of a so-called *"open"* post-mill can be clearly seen. However, often the lower part is completely or partially covered. This is known as a *"closed"* or "*half closed"* post-mill. Post mills are still to be seen in the provinces of Groningen, Overijssel, Gelderland, Zeeland, Noord-Brabant and Limburg, and there is one in Zuid-Holland.

Post-mill in Rosmalen (1732)

Next page:
main picture: *Post-mill "Retranchement", Zeeland*
right: *Post-mill, Bourtange*
left: *Post-mill, Heusden*

Hollow post-mill

"Grosmolen", Hoogmade

"De rooie Wip", Hazerswoude

This type has evolved from the post-mill. The rectangular mill house has been made smaller and the pyramid shaped lower part has been made bigger (higher). The post has been changed to a strong hollow post which supports the mill house.

"Vlietmolen", Meerkerk

Most wip mills are draining mills and they can mainly be found in Zuid-Holland (about 80), West-Utrecht and western Noord-Brabant. There is a smaller type of wip mill in the province of Friesland called *"Spinnekop"*.

Groenedijkse mill (1627)

Large mill, Zoeterwoude, 17th century

"De kleine molen", Stiens (Friesland)

Grassland mill on the Zaanse Schans

MEADOW MILL OR "AANBRENGERTJE"

The meadow mill or *"Aanbrengertje"* is a drainage mill as well but its work is restricted. It brings the water from low lying parts to ditches on the general level of that polder. These mills are comparatively small and are mainly to be seen in the province of Noord-Holland.

Hollow post-mill in Weerribben

The Tjasker

A "Tjasker" in Wijckel (Friesland)

The Tjasker is another small polder mill which is used for draining as well as for the irrigation of reed land. The construction, however, is entirely different from the usual type of mill.
It is made of one long axle where, on one side the sails are attached and on the other (under) side there is a helix (screw of Archimedes) surrounded by a wooden cylinder, the barrel. The Tjasker is a mill that is turned as a whole. Tjaskers could originally only be seen in Friesland and Noord-Overijssel and depending on the construction, are named a pole or trestle Tjasker.

"De gekroonde Poelenburg", Zaanse Schans

The Paltrok

The Paltrok is another mill that is turned into the wind in its entirety but that is the only thing it has in common with the above mentioned mill. The type originated and has been further developed in the Zaan area where, at one time, they appeared in great numbers. They are exclusively timber saw mills, closed only at the front (windward) while the protruding sides (wings) and back are open.
When these mills were built there were Mennonite refugees in Holland who came from the German Palz area. The tail coats these people wore were of a particular design and this style of coat was generally worn then, hence the name *"Palz-rock"* (Palz-coat). Because the outline of this coat resembled that of the mills, the mills too became

Interior of a Paltrok mill "De Otter"

"De held Jozua", Zaandam

known as Palz-rocks, which name through common usage came to be Paltrok. Unfortunately of all the hundreds of Paltrok mills that used to adorn the landscape, there are only 4 still in existence.

"De Eenhoorn", Haarlem

Ground-sailers

Ground-sailers are to be found in places where there is little or nothing to obstruct the wind.
They are built directly at ground level and therefore also operated from the ground.
In Friesland one often sees ground-sailers/top-wheelers which drain the polders and are called *"monks' mills"*.

"Moppe Molen" in Nieuwe Wetering in the year 1752

"Oudkerkermolen", Oudkerk (Friesland)

Smock Mills with a stage

"De Rat", IJlst (Friesland)

If in the vicinity of a site where one intended to build a mill, obstacles in the shape of tall buildings or trees were near, one made the windmill high enough to catch the wind. In order to be able to adjust the sailcloth, to turn it into the wind and to apply the brake , a stage or platform was built around the mill. The lower part was generally used as an extra store-room. This type of mill is easily recognised by its height and stage. This is especially true when they rise 33 metres above ground level, as is the case with the five windmills in Schiedam.

Next page: main picture: *"De Graen Halm", Haamstede* ***above:*** *Tower mill, Sloten* ***centre:*** *Tower mills, Schiedam* ***below:*** *"Wolzigd", Roderwolde (1852)*

The Leidschendam mills

"Berg" or Belt Mills

The earthen mound built up around these mills has the same function as the stage for the smock mills. This berg (mound) or belt is used to adjust the sails, the turning mechanism and the brake.

At one side, at ground level, there is a tunnelled entrance and exit for raw materials and products. Nearly all of these are corn mills.

"De Heimolen", St. Hubert

Mountain mill "St. Viktor", Heeze

"De Oude Grafelijke Korenmolen", Zeddam in the year 1450 (Gelderland)

Tower Mills

This brick cylindrical mill was possibly introduced into Holland by the crusaders who encountered such mills in countries around the Mediterranean.
They were never in great numbers and now there are only 4 left in our country.

"Moppe molen", Nieuwe Wetering (1752)

HEXAGONAL OR OCTAGONAL TOP-WHEELERS

A group of various windmills fall under this name. They all have in common the fact that the top part, the cap, can be turned to face the wind. The top-wheeler/inner-wheeler of which the turning mechanism is inside the cap can mainly be found in the province of Noord-Holland (for example Schermer, Zijpe and Haze polders).

They are sturdy, heavy, octagonal mills which look very well indeed in the rather bare scenery of the Noord-Holland polder landscape.

The cap of the top-wheeler/outer-wheeler is also turned to set the sails facing the wind, but the actual turning is done outside the mill.

Smock windmills, Schermerhorn

Octagonal and Round Brick Top-wheelers

These are brick built, round or octagonal windmills. Because of the weight of their building materials these mills are not seen so often in the west of the country because of the soft ground.

"Windvang", Goedereede

Mills, Kinderdijk

How does a

1. Stock
2. Sail
3. Bearing
4. Brake wheel
5. Windshaft
6. Staves wheel
7. Brake
8. Luffing gear
9. Brake lever
10. Hoist
11. Main axle
12. Spur wheel
13. Quant
14. Casing with stones
15. Meal spout
16. Stage door

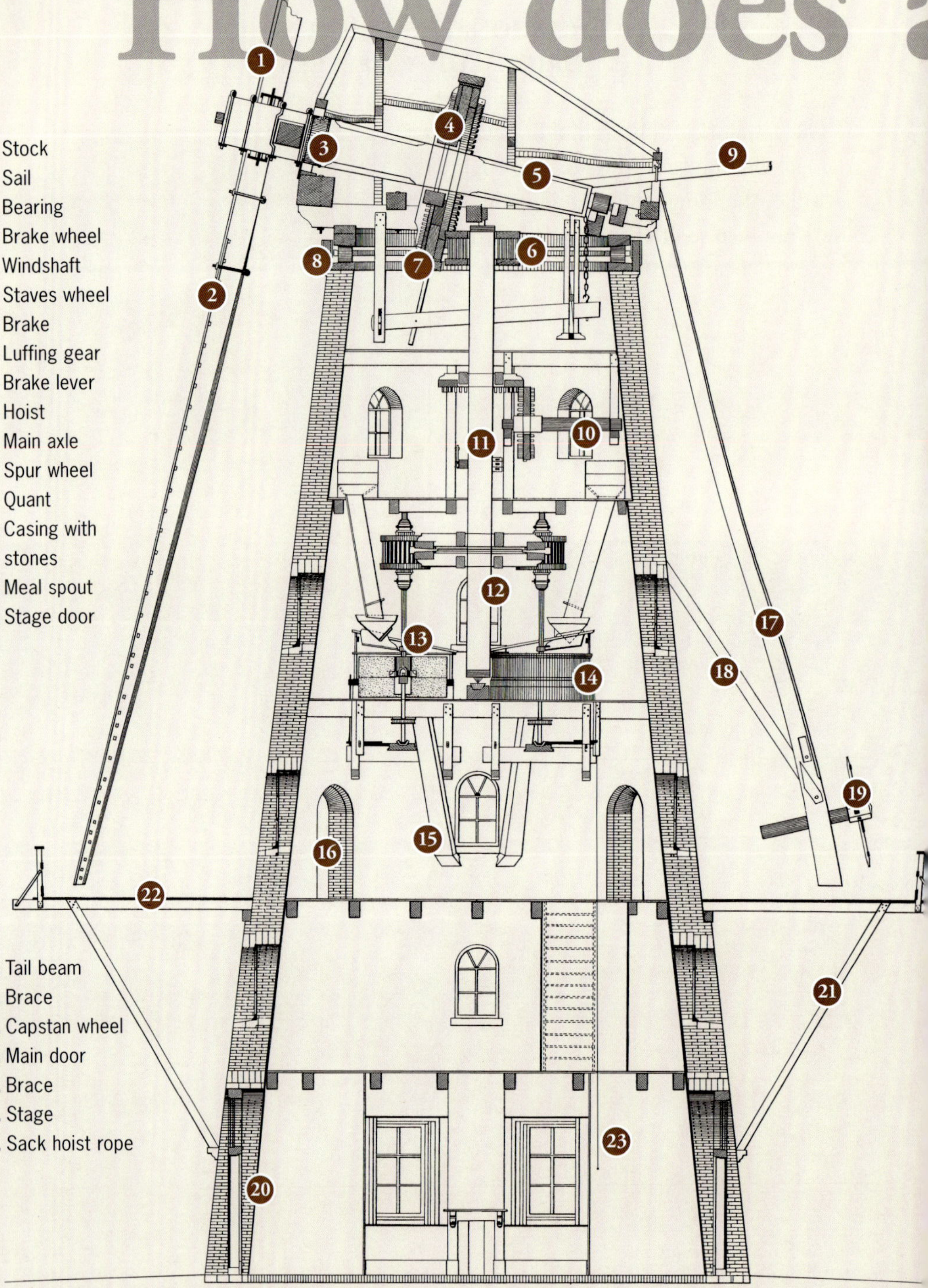

17. Tail beam
18. Brace
19. Capstan wheel
20. Main door
21. Brace
22. Stage
23. Sack hoist rope

mill work?

1. Windshaft
2. Sail
3. Brake wheel
4. Brake lever
5. Brace
6. Capstan wheel
7. Tail beam
8. Upright shaft
9. Screw
10. Under spill wheel
11. Drain
12. Gate door

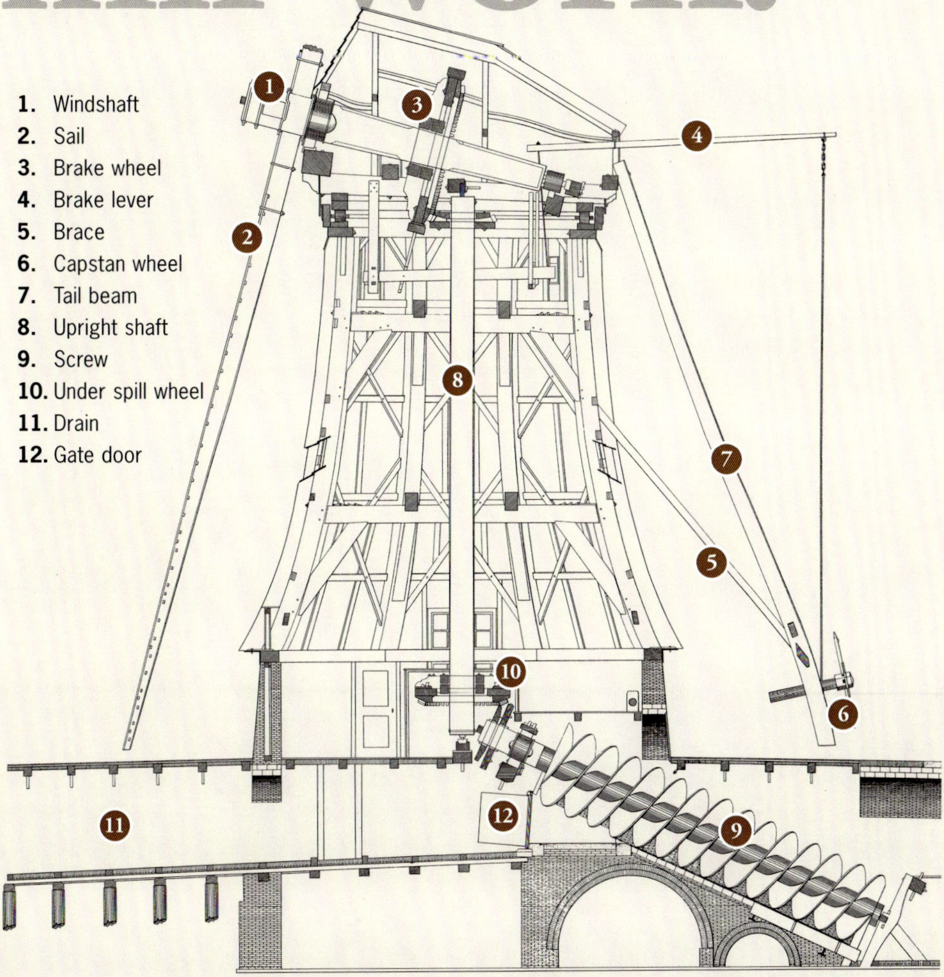

The energy source of the windmill is the wind, which drives the sails. The sails are attached to the windshaft. Round the windshaft there is a brake wheel that turns along with it and conveys the movement to the wallower which is connected to the upright shaft to which one or more wheels are fastened. By studying illustration II of the watermill you will get a fairly good idea of the working of a windmill. Depending on the force of the wind, the sail-cloth is fully or partially set, and after lifting the brake (brake shoes around the brake wheel) with the brake lever, the mill can start turning. It goes without saying that it needs to face the wind and has to be adjusted. This is done by turning the mill.

The majority of mills have a turning device that can be seen from the outside with a capstan wheel or turning winch, except the inner-wheelers which have their turning mechanism inside the cap.

A series of stepped drainage mills

When the difference between the water level in the polder and that of the *"boezemwater"* (surrounding storage water) is too great and cannot be coped with by one single drainage mill, then a series of mills is placed in a row. As soon as the total of the drainage levels of this series of mills is sufficient to come from polder level to *"boezem"* level one has achieved one's goal. Each mill in turn lifts the water one *"step"* up. The name of this system is *"stepped drainage"* and the row of mills, a series (molengang). When there are three mills it is called a *"three series"*, and four mills, a *"four series"*.
The system can be clearly seen from the drawing.

main picture: *Series of windmills, Leidschendam*
above right: *Series of windmills, Schermerhorn*
below right: *Series of windmills, Kinderdijk*

1. The *"upright position"* (with one sail-arm in front of the mill) or *"working position"* indicates a short period of rest. When they are not in operation, the mills are almost always in this position. The sail-arms are in a horizontal and vertical position, making it easy to conduct any necessary (maintenance) work to the sail-arms. Nowadays, one can observe that the mills are usually in this position, as it is then easier to fit the mill with a lightning conductor.

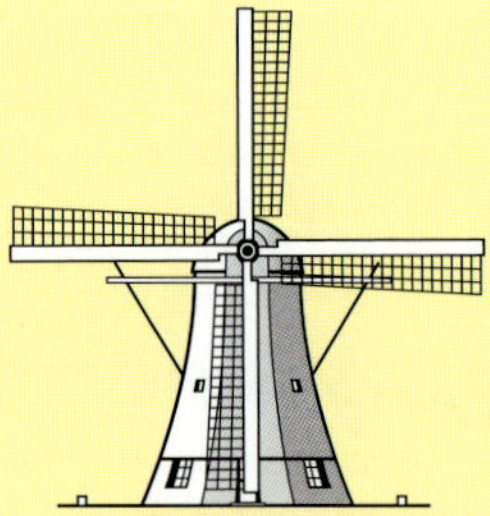

2. The *"diagonal"* or *"cross over"* position is the position that indicates a longer period of rest. The cross that is formed by the sails is at a 45 degree angle with the horizon. The sail-arms are in the lowest possible position and are therefore least likely to be struck by lightning.

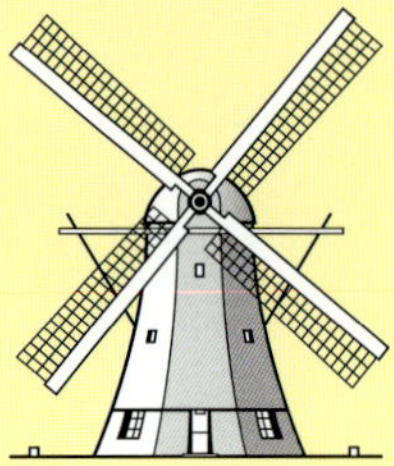

3. The *"rejoicing position"* indicates that the miller's family has something to celebrate, for example a wedding or a birth. In this position, the approaching (descending) sail-arm is stopped just before it reaches its lowest point. The fact that the sail-arm is *"approaching"* symbolises the joy and expectation. (In the Province of Noord-Brabant however, this position is used to indicate a time of mourning.)

4. The *"mourning position"* indicates sadness and mourning. In this case, the *"departing"* sail-arm is stopped just after it leaves its lowest point. The fact that the sail-arm is *"departing"* expresses mortality, and sadness. (Once again, this position expresses exactly the opposite, namely joy, in Noord-Brabant.)

5. The sail-arms of the mills in the Netherlands always rotate to the left, counter-clockwise.

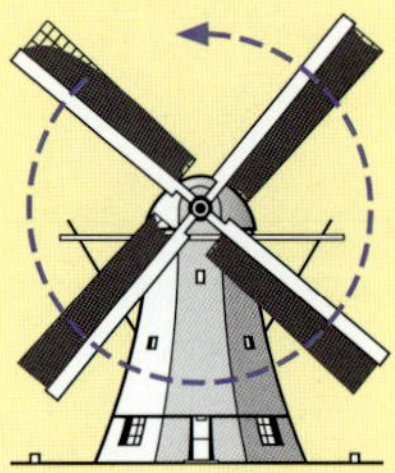

Mill Language

Sometimes one notices that mills at rest do not always have their sails in the same position. The reason for this being that the miller wishes to communicate with the neighbourhood. The mill was always the centre of the community and the miller was informed by his customers of the local news. If there was a reason for celebration then the miller would signify this by stopping the sail just before it reached its highest position, this is called *"coming"*. The mill sails always turn anti-clockwise. This coming position occurs when there is a birth, marriage or some similar joyful event. If, however, the vertical sail has just passed its highest point, *"going"*, then it means someone has died and that the miller is in mourning. If the sails are in a pure horizontal and vertical position, this indicates that the miller is resting for a brief period and intends to resume work shortly. If, however, the sails form an "X" cross, so at 45 degrees to the vertical and horizontal position, the miller indicates that he is resting for a longer period. The mill then rests in a *'cross over'* position.

This position will not be seen very often nowadays. Because mills are now fitted with lightning conductors there is no longer the need to set the sails in the cross over position which makes the mill lower in order to lessen the risk of it being struck by lightning.
The miller also used certain resting positions to signal messages to confidants. For instance, to let the millwright know that his services were required. During wartime too, messages were relayed by prearranged signals and in World War II they were frequently used to warn people in hiding, etc. about raids.

6 & 7. A mill *"adorned in celebration"* for special occasions (for example a wedding), including flags and decorations. The *"rejoicing position"* is also used on these occasions. It is also called the *"Whitsun position"*.

DECORATING

Oukopermolen in the year 1839

In the Zaan region (just north of Amsterdam) the custom is to deck the mill out for weddings and wedding celebrations of the miller or his family, although there is no strict uniformity in decorating. These photos show examples; the decorated sails are set to face the festive house. The summer and winter sailcloths are rolled up lengthwise and plaited into the sails. Stretched between the wing tips is a rope entwined with fir twigs. In the middle are the initials of the bridal couple, and perhaps, as on the picture the number of years the couple has been married. Trumpet angels (the Fame) perched on the wing tips announce the celebrated event.

From the sail tips, hanging down on the ropes are a hoop on which Cupid's two love arrows are crossed, and protectively held in love's open heart, two tiny tin *'mills'* that gently sway to the music of the wind, as they reflect the sun's glittering rays.
Small houses of open lattice-work represent marriage cages. The couple stand with outstretched arms as if they are going to meet each other, the bridegroom on the left and the bride on the right. Their cages symbolise the end of their *'freedom'*. A multi-pointed-star or sun represents happiness. Underneath is a bridal crown. On the top left and right wings are hearts (love) and on the bottom left and right a ring (the universal symbol of the conjugal band). And of course, the windmill proudly displays the Dutch flag!

"De Graanhalm", Haamstede

Next page: main picture: *Mill "De Kat" ,*
inset: *"De gekroonde Poelenburg" both in Zaandam*

Wind Turbines

Windmills have been a familiar sight in the Dutch landscape for many centuries. After the number of mills had been reduced from 9,000 to around 1,000, this trend was reversed in the 1970s to an increase.

Modern wind turbines also appeared on the horizon, mainly along dikes and on wide open spaces. These wind turbines are built to supply (clean) energy which they generate from wind power.

The designs are the result of modern technology, and when there is sufficient wind, these mills can provide power for a whole residential estate.

Windmills near Lelystad

Windmills near St. Maartensburg

Visits to mills

Hundreds of volunteer millers work to ensure that numerous mills are in operation from time to time. It is usually possible to visit these mills on Saturdays, though another day of the week is occasionally possible as well. The miller then hoists 'the blue ribbon'. A limited number of mills is open during most of the year and during certain hours. The second Saturday in May is our national Mill Day. Any mill that can turn its sails is then in operation. Flour and the like can be bought at many of the flourmills.

Interior of "De Kat" in Zaandam

The mills on the Zaanse Schans

Colophon

Text	C.P. Braaij
Composition	Herman Scholten, Willem Kooijman, Philipp E. van Ekeren
Photography	Herman Scholten
Design/lay-out/illustrations	Tjasker Design Amsterdam
Publishing/Distribution	Kooijman Souvenirs & Gifts bv
ISBN	90-71816-02-8

The Kinderdijk mills